The Fox and the Ducks

Written by Jill Atkins
Illustrated by Natascha Rosenberg

Fox runs to the ducks.

He unzips his bag.

Quack! Quack!
It is the fox.

5

Bugs buzz at Fox.

Fox yaps at the bugs.

He gets stuck in the mud!

9

Yes, let's help Fox.

The ducks go to Fox.

13

The ducks quack at Fox.

Fox runs.

He zips up his bag.